# THE BOOK OF RUTH

# A Bible Study

## For Group or Individual Study

### By Patsy Scott

# THE BOOK OF RUTH
## BIBLE STUDY

# BACKGROUND INFORMATION

There are 66 listed books in the Bible. Only two are named after women (Esther being the other book.) The book of Ruth is respected as a true historical narrative.In the genealogy listing of Jesus, only 4 women are mentioned: Tamar, Rahab, Bathsheba, and Ruth.

Ruth contains several themes and messages, among a few being: loss and restoration, repentance, redemption, and new birth. The book of Ruth also brings home the truth that being a part God's family is decided, not by blood, but by the surrender and alignment of one's heart and life to the will of God through an obedience that comes from faith.

The time setting for the book of Ruth is actually a time of peace rather than the typical war that pervaded the "time of the judges". And Israel and Moab, the two nations in the story, are temporarily at peace.

Being it is the time of judges (Ruth 1:1) that this story takes place, it is a unique and unusual story giving us a different perspective of this era. Rather than darkness, we see rays of light. Rather that faithlessness, we see faith.

By the 6th century, Ruth was being used liturgically at Pentecost. (Celebration of the Harvest). Its location in the Bible is historical, and between Judges and Samuel. [4]

Today, the Book of Ruth is read in Jewish synagogues during Shavuot. Shavuot "commemorates the revelation of the Torah on Mt. Sinai to the Jewish people, and occurs on the 50th day after the 49 days of counting the Omer." (2017 Shavout was May 30-June 1). Shavuot is associated with the grain harvest in the Torah. [1]

There are three Jewish explanations why Ruth is read during Shavuot:

1. Ruth's coming to Israel took place around the time of Shavuot. Her acceptance into the Jewish faith was like the acceptance of the Jewish people of God's Torah.[2]

2. Because there is a legend that David died on Shavuot and the book of Ruth ends with the genealogy of David. [2]

3. The story of Ruth takes place at harvest time, and Shavuot also occurs at the time of the spring harvest. [2]

Author

Some bible scholars think possibly Samuel was the author (The Talmud, c. AD 200)[3], but since Samuel died before David's reign, and the book of Ruth refers to David's kingdom, this is questionable - unless someone finished the writing for him. Many bible scholars agree that Ruth was likely written in the time of David's reign or anytime there after. The literary style used is Hebrew typical of that time.[3] Whoever the author was, they did a great job of revealing God's desire to bless 'all peoples on earth' (Genesis 12:3). [4]

Time of the Judges

The span of the judges is approximately 200 years (1250-1050 B.C.) and falls between the death of Joshua (coming into the promise land) and the reign of King Saul. (King David followed Saul). The time of the judges was a time of apostasy, moral degradation, and oppression. It was a dark and bloody era. There was this recurring cycle by Israel: disobedience, foreign oppression, cries of distress, then deliverance. For instance, in Canaan, Israel quickly forgot the acts of God that had given her birth and had established her in the land. The Israelites instead settled down and attached themselves to Canaan's peoples, their morals, their gods, and their religious beliefs and practices. Therefore, God's hand came upon them in the form of foreign oppression. Eventually Israel would cry out to the Lord, and the Lord would give deliverance through a judge. [4]

There were 12 judges for Israel. Out of the 12, these five were renown for bringing great deliverance to the people of Israel:

| | |
|---|---|
| Ehud | defeated the Moabites |
| Deborah | defeated the Canaanites |
| Gideon | defeated the Medianites |
| Jephthah | defeated the Ammonites |
| Samson | challenged the Philistines |

Names

In biblical times, a persons name had meaning.

| | |
|---|---|
| Elimelech: | God is King |
| Naomi: | Pleasant, beautiful, agreeable |
| Mahlon: | Weakling, infirmity |
| Kilion (or Chilion): | Finished, complete |
| Ruth: | Friendship, satisfied |
| Orpah: | Fawn or neck |
| Boaz: | In strength |

Moab

The hills of Moab can be seen from Bethlehem to the east across the Dead Sea. Though near to Israel, Moab was not friendly territory. The Moabites were descended from Lot (Genesis 19:27) and so were distant relatives of Israel. However, they had been hostile when the Israelites had approached from Egypt after the exodus (Numbers 21:29). Early in the period of the judges, Eglon King of Moab had invaded and dominated the Israelites for 18 years. [4] The book of Ruth reflects a temporary time of peace between Israel and Moab.

Famine in the Bible

Famine was God's judgment for unfaithfulness in Israel. (Deut. 28:17, 23, 38-40, 42). As well, famine was used to advance God's plans. (Gen. 12:10, 26:1, 41-50). The famine in Ruth is not mentioned in the book of Judges. Nor is there mention of a mass exodus in the book of Ruth due to a famine. However, Elimelech and his family left their home because of famine.

As you do your study, be sure and check the appendix for lesson notes and helps.

# LESSON 1

# Being Made Empty

# Ruth 1:1-7

**God's Way of Getting Us Home**

Before beginning Lesson 1, it would serve well to first
read the entire book of Ruth.


## Lesson 1 Introduction

Ruth 1:1-7 sets the scene and conditions to Ruth's story and introduces us to the characters. In these first seven verses, we are introduced to a family – a family who has made a major decision that will radically change their life. The result of that decision was an emptying.

The story begins with Naomi. She and her husband, Elimelech, together made the decision to leave Israel for Moab. But now Naomi, less her husband and her sons, broken and empty, makes another life-changing decision. This time it is to return home.

This decision, to *return*, is a crucial moment for Naomi. The Hebrew word (shwub) used for "return" is also the Hebrew word used for "repent." [1] Being made empty, Naomi repented; she returned! This is the heart of Lesson 1.

 The journey from Moab to Bethlehem, their return, would be about 50 miles. The journey was one of navigating a rugged and rough terrain. If they walked about 8 hours in a day, resting at night, it would have taken them a bit over one week. They would have left Moab, traveling north until they reached where the Jordan River meets the Dead Sea. Here they would cross and then travel west and finally south to Bethlehem.

Map taken from:
https://www.thebiblejourney.org/content/pages/uploaded_images/959.jpg

## LESSON 1
### Ruth 1:1-7

**OPENING QUESTION**

Negative situations stir us to want to make a change. We can move away, change jobs, stop doing something, or start doing something to fix that negative in our life. Can you think of a time this occurred in your life? What were the conditions and what change did you choose to make?

**LEAVING (vs. 1-2)**

In these two verses, we are introduced to the family of Elimelech. We are told their present economic condition (famine), their hometown (Bethlehem), their names and most importantly, their major life changing decision to move away. Be sure to read the introductory notes to Ruth then answer these questions.

1. Not knowing what lay ahead, what pros and cons might this family have listed in deciding to move to Moab?
   Pros                         Cons

2. This is pure speculation, but how might you describe Elimelech's spiritual condition at this time-- based on your answers to question 1?

3. Which of these three choices would you say best explains this family's decision? (Circle your choice).

    a.   They did the weak thing by leaving and not persevering through the famine.

    b.   They made a wise decision to leave and come back later.

    c.   They left more than just Bethlehem.

4. If they were leaving more than just Bethlehem, what would that be?

**PRESSURE (vs. 3-5)**
You can read about the Moabites and the Ammonites in Genesis 19:30-36. These two nations became bitter enemies of Abraham's descendants. (1 Samuel 14:47; 2 Chronicles 20:1) To marry a Moabite was not ideal for a Jew for no Moabite, or his sons to the tenth generation, was allowed to "enter the assembly of the Lord" (Deut. 23:3). We can understand then how a devout Jew might think toward the Moabite people. Hence, for Elimelech to choose to move to Moab, and later for his sons to marry Moabite women gives us much insight into Elimelech as head of this family.

1. Elimelech means "God is King" which tells us something about the beliefs of the Israelites and says something about Elimelech's parents who named him. What does it say to you?

2. Elimelech named his two sons, who were born in Bethlehem, Mahlon (meaning infirmity) and Kilion (meaning finished, complete). What might these names tell us about their years in Bethlehem?

3. In verse 1, we are told that this family intended to move to Moab just temporarily. In verse 3 we find it is now 10 years later. If you were Naomi and were writing a letter home, summing up the last 10 years, what might be the good things as well as the sad things she would write in her letter?

4. We see there were hard times in Bethlehem and there were harder times in Moab. I Timothy 6:10 says: *Some people, eager for money, have wandered from the faith and pierced themselves with many griefs* Do you think this verse is applicable? Why or why not?

5. What have been *your* emptying experiences and what did you learn?

## DECISION to RETURN  (vs. 6-7)
1. While in Moab, what was it Naomi heard about back home?

2. What good things did you hear about the Lord that drew you to Him?

3. Empty stomachs desire food. Naomi heard that there was food again in Bethlehem but we know there was also food in Moab. What is at the heart of this?

4. What is your spiritual food and what has it meant to your life?

5. Verse 6 is the turning point for Naomi. She "heard," and then she "prepared." Then they set out. A woman alone, ready to embark on a long trip. What now do you think of Naomi?

6. Use verse 7 of Ruth Chapter 1 quoted here to fill in the blanks in the second quoting of the same verse.

*With her two daughters-in-law, she left the place where she had been living and set out on the road that would take them back to the land of Judah.*

With her two daughters-in-law, she _____ the _____ where she had been _____ and set out on the _____ that would take them _____ to the land of Judah.

Which of the fill-ins stand out to you the most and why?

7. Think about what Naomi was leaving and what she was returning to. On the road back Naomi will have lots of time to think. Describe some thoughts you would have if you were Naomi on the road, returning.

## REPENTANCE

1. What does "repentance" mean to you? Explain it in your own words.

2. Why can we look at Naomi's returning as a repentance?

3. Do you have a story of repentance the Lord might want you to share with the group?

## CLOSING

1. What do you see as the difference for this family between leaving Bethlehem for Moab and leaving Moab for Bethlehem.

2.  Which move do you think was the hardest?  Why?

**LIFE APPLICATION:**
Going back. In our spiritual journey, the Lord is always willing to take us back and very much *wants* us back when we have strayed. It may be back to church, back to prayer, back to the Bible, back to right relationships. What might you say to someone who has been away from the church, from Christian fellowship, or that personal relationship with the Lord for some time, and they are now at a very hollow place, empty like Naomi?

**WHAT DID YOU LEARN?**

# LESSON 2

# Ruth 1:8-18

# Irresistible Love

**A Pledge of Love**

Lesson 2 Introduction

In Lesson 2 we look at Orpah and Ruth. Both are good women and both
love their mother-in-law, but only one found love irresistible.


As we study this section of Ruth, we want to discover what irresistible
love is. We will look deep into Ruth's pledge of love and commitment
and our own Christian love and commitment. We will also consider
Orpah and why she did not pledge her love as Ruth did.



To further prepare, please read Deuteronomy 25:5-6

# LESSON 2
## Ruth 1:8-18

**OPENING QUESTIONS**

Do you remember trying to talk your mother into letting you do something? What were some of your promises you made so she would give in?

As a mother, what promises from your child would convince you that they would stand by their words?

**OPTIONS (vs. 8-9a)**

1. Naomi prays a blessing over her daughters-in-law. What are the two things Naomi asks of the Lord for her daughters-in-law?

2. These blessing tell us what about Naomi's relationship with the Lord?

3. Describe, from these verses (8, 9) Naomi's daughters-in-law.

4. Naomi wishes that Orpah and Ruth would find *rest* in the home of another husband. This is a nice wish for them, isn't it? But because we have read the whole book of Ruth, we know that something good lay ahead in *Bethlehem*. If Naomi had understood this what might she have said instead?

19

5. At this point, Orpah and Ruth had not converted to Judaism. Why not do you think? What might be the story?

## The "WISDOM of the WORLD" and the "PULL OF REASONING" (vs. 9b-13)

1. What are Naomi's reasons that the girls should remain with their families? Is she right?

2. What does Naomi's encouraging the girls to stay in Moab say about her hope for the future?

3. Hope is wonderful, but when we don't have it, we can't really pass it on. When was a time you needed hope and someone helped you gain it?

4. Look at these three verses and make application to either Ruth, Oprah or Naomi and their words about going or staying.

   Genesis 3:1-6

   Proverbs 3:5

   I Corinthians 1:18-21

## TWO DIFFERENT DECISIONS  (vs. 14-18)

1. Pretend you are Orpah and tell why you made the choice you did. Then pretend you are Ruth, and tell why you did what you did.

   Orpah:


   Ruth:


2. In verse 15 we see Orpah will return to two things. What are they? Your thoughts?




3. Ruth decides to go with Naomi and chooses Naomi's God as well. This is the moment of Ruth's conversion to the one true God. (Look at John 6:60-71 for further thought). Why do you think Orpah didn't make the same choice? Why was Ruth different?




4. Orpah kissed her mother-in-law goodbye; Ruth clung to her (v. 14). What a beautiful and precise picture of one choosing life and the other not though she thought she was choosing life. Read Matthew 10:39. Does the story of Ruth help you understand this scripture? How so?




5. We see here the power of irresistible love when Ruth clings to Naomi. The same word *cling* is used in Genesis 2:24 where a man leaves father and mother and clings to his wife. What would cause us to cling to the Lord as Ruth is clinging to Naomi?

6. Read Ephesians 3:17b-19. Why do Christians follow Christ with different intensities? Why did you follow Christ as you do?

7. Look at Ruth's pledges of commitment to Naomi, and to God. They are the same as a Christian's commitment to Christ.

I will go - Ruth is willing to leave behind the old life.
Where you stay, I will stay - Ruth is willing to take up a new life.
Your people, will be my people – Ruth is willing to love and join with the people of God.
Where you die, I will die – Ruth's commitment is forever

Have you made all four pledges, yourself, to the Lord? What is your story?

**CLOSING**
If you were to make a fresh pledge to God today, what would you say?

**WHAT DID YOU LEARN?**

# Lesson 3

# Ruth 1:19-22

# Honesty

**Pouring it out!**

Lesson 3 Introduction

In this lesson we will see:

Naomi and Ruth coming back to Bethlehem and being greeted by the people.

Naomi giving her sad testimony covering the last 10 years of her life; she tells them not to call her Naomi (pleasant, agreeable) but to call her Mara (bitter).

Naomi is honest with her people and with God. She does not pretend to be pleasant or agreeable with life as her name signifies. No! She tells it like it is. She is real.

But he truth will set us free! (John 8:32). Something is about to change Naomi and Ruth's lives – it is barley harvest time!

## LESSON 3
Ruth 1:19-22

**OPENING QUESTION**

Sometimes we need someone to pour our hearts out to. Is there anyone you would trust to do this with and why them?

**NAOMI"S FACE  (v. 19)**

1. Naomi gets a wonderful reception. She has come home and the whole town is stirred and excited about it. Why does the town respond this way?

2. Our faces can tell where we've been, what has happened to us, and what we are feeling. It's been 10 years and Naomi has aged, but what else might they see in her face that they would exclaim, "Can this be Naomi?"

   What is the significance of this?

3. What was Naomi's initial need when arriving in Bethlehem and how did the people meet it?

**HONESTY (vs. 20-21)**

1. Naomi lost a husband and then two sons while in Moab. In verses 20 and 21, she spiels out some very strong statements, using  words like:

bitter, empty, afflicted, misfortune, and "The Lord has testified against me." Is she wrong to say these things? Explain.

2. Some people, when angry or disappointed with God, can tell him so. Others just can't do that and in fact see it as wrong. Why? Which are you?

3. Based on Naomi's story, how would she describe God and His heart toward her at this point?
   a. Stern and unhappy with her.
   b. Just waiting to hold her, comfort her and bless her.
   c. Distant but watching.
   d. _____

   What is the truth?

## IT'S BARLEY HARVEST TIME! (v. 22)
Read Jeremiah 29: 10-13. The prophet Jeremiah is speaking this to the people of Israel who were taken into captivity for 70 years because of their sin as a nation. Here, God is telling Israel His heart, what He truly wishes for them and what He will do for them at the end of their captivity.

1. Naomi's time in a foreign land is over, but she still feels God's displeasure. According to Jeremiah 29:11 what is the true intent of God toward the returning and repentant Naomi?

2. Jeremiah 29:10-13 is also God's heart towards us. What are you going through or feeling today that you can apply this promise to?

3. Read Isaiah 54:4-8 and use this passage to speak hope to Naomi, in your own words. What would you say?

4. In Ruth 1:8-9 Naomi prayed for the Lord's kindness to be upon her daughters-in law. Then Ruth shows Naomi a wonderful kindness by going with Naomi to her home. More kindnesses await both Naomi and Ruth and, in fact, the next kindness is right before them: the barley fields are ready for harvest. Perfect timing! Can you tell of a barley field in your life that you just didn't see at first and wasn't expecting? What was it? Why didn't you see it?

**CLOSING**
The story will next shift to Ruth. In verse 22 we are reminded that she is a Moabitess.

1. What is the significance of being reminded that Ruth is a Moabite?

2. Have you ever felt like a Moabitess in a new or different place? What happened?

**WHAT DID YOU LEARN?**

# LESSON 4

# Ruth 2:1-13

# Under His Wings

**He extends His favor to us and abundantly provides
for those who acknowledge His name!**

## Lesson 4 Introduction

In Chapter 2 of Ruth we are introduced to Boaz. His name means "in Him is strength." This is the man who can bless these women. He is the "Christ" figure in this beautiful analogy of God's plan to save and bless us.

Blessing and favor is waiting for Naomi and Ruth. But let's look at something: Naomi, though she knows of this "mighty man of wealth" (KJ) and that he is a relative, doesn't take advantage of that when first coming back to Bethlehem. Ruth, on the other hand, does not know who this man is, but because she and Naomi must eat, she goes to the fields hoping to find *favor* with someone. She comes upon the fields of Boaz. She is right where God wants her! Right where God can extend blessing and favor. Why does God extend favor to these two women? That is what we are to discover in Lesson 4.

# LESSON 4
Ruth 2:1-13

---

**OPENING QUESTION**
Was there anyone in your life, growing up, who took special interest in you? Maybe they made you feel good about yourself or looked out for you, but they somehow favored you? Tell us about it.

**BOAZ (v. 1)**
1. What are the two things we are told about Boaz?

2. Have you ever considered thinking of Jesus as that rich and influential relative? Explain whatt these verses say to reinfoce this mind set.

   II Cor. 8:9

   II Cor. 9:10-11

   Romans 8:16-17

**DIRECTED FOOTSTEPS (vs. 2-3)**
1. We can't overlook Ruth's humbling circumstances, that she is a foreigner, reduced to poverty and a gleaner in the fields. What do you *most* admire about Ruth?
   _ Her courage and willingness to take risks
   _ Her work ethic
   _ Her humble spirit
   _ Her loyalty to those she loved

   Why?

2.  Ruth not only wanted to pick up grain, but was hoping to find favor with the owner of a field.  What is she saying about "finding favor" and why does she wish for it?

3.  Ruth is picking up *leftover* grain.  In John 6, after feeding the 5000 with one fish and two barley loafs, Jesus gave instructions to pick up the leftovers that nothing would be wasted.  What does this mean?  Who are the leftovers meant for?

4.  Ruth finds herself in the fields of the relative, Boaz, mentioned in verse 1.  We know this isn't by chance or by luck, but by the Spirit of God guiding her footsteps.  Often, we don't see the hand of God when it is there at work, but when we look back we realize God's gracious and wise hands were upon us. Do you have a story in this regard?

**A GOOD RECOMMENDATION (vs. 4-7)**
1. Boaz's greeting is more like what we might hear in church, not the work place. What does this tell us about Boaz, other than he believes in God?

2. In verses 5-7, the foreman gives three good recommendations about Ruth. What are they?

_____
_____
_____

Why would these be so important for Boaz to hear?

3. The foreman spoke good words into Boaz's ears causing favor to be given to Ruth. YOU, too, are highly favored – by God. But what is it like to receive His favor? Think about how you would treat someone who you highly favored. In light of that, name some ways God might show you favor?


## HIS WORDS (vs. 8-9)

1. God's Word gives us specific instructions how we are to lead a Christian life. When we follow them we will be blessed and protected. Boaz gives Ruth three specific instructions. Take those instructions and make spiritual application for your own life. (An example is given for the first.)

   - Stay with my servant girls in my field
     Application: We are to fellowship with fellow believers.
     (Your) Application:

   - Follow my girls and keep your eyes on this field
     Application:

   - When you are thirsty, go and get a drink from my water jars
     Application:


## REASON FOR GOD'S GRACE and FAVOR (vs. 10-11)

1. Ruth asked Boaz "Why have I found such favor in your eyes?" What is the answer?


2. What are some reasons we find favor with God? (read Psalm 5:11-12, John 1:12; Proverbs 8:34-35)

## A BLESSING PRAYER (v. 12)
1. Boaz extends wonderful favor toward Ruth, for which she is humbly grateful. What do you most admire about Boaz? Why?

       \_\_ His rapport with his workers
       \_\_ His respect for a foreign woman
       \_\_ His generosity with his grain
       \_\_ His protection of Ruth
       \_\_ Other _____

2. Boaz prays a blessing over Ruth (v 12). It is more than a pious wish, he really wants her to be richly rewarded, and her faith strengthened by seeing all her needs met. He ends with saying that she has come and taken refuge under the God of Israel's wings. In this season, Boaz will become God's wings over Ruth and Naomi. Let's better grasp how God desires to be covering wings over us.

   Look up these "wing" passages. Then pick the one one that blesses you the most. Tell us why it blesses you.

   Psalm 17:5-8          Psalm 91:4          Luke 13:34

   _____
   _____
   _____
   _____
   _____
   _____

3. Is there any responsibility on our part to "be covered by his wings?"

34

## HUMILITY (v. 13)

1. Ruth humbly thanks Boaz. Use her words as a model and write out your own prayer of gratitude to God, who covers you with His wings.

_____

_____

_____

_____

_____

## DEEPER

1. In the book of Ruth, the foreman is symbolic of the Holy Spirit speaking favor into the ears of the one who can bless her. Jeremiah 29:11 talks about God's desire to bless you and give you a future. I Samuel 2:26 and Luke 2:52 mention favor with man as well as with God. Based on these, consider where you are in need of favor. (Maybe with your employer, a co-worker, your spouse, an unsaved friend you'd like to witness to). With whom do you want to ask God to give you favor?

2. As you end this session of study, pray for one another, asking for His favor to extend into your specific situation. Or each individual may voice his own prayer and request to God, and the others stand in agreement.

## WHAT DID YOU LEARN?

# LESSON 5

# Ruth 2:14-23

# Breaking Bread

**An Offer of Fellowship**

## Lesson 5 Introduction

Boaz invites Ruth, the foreigner, to eat with him and his workers. This is not a small gesture. In fact, it bears deeper meaning than just a meal.

Reminiscent to us of the Lord's table, Boaz gives Ruth bread and vinegar wine. Then he makes it possible for Ruth to be blessed above her expectations. In this lesson, we see the importance of actions. We will think about Boaz's actions, God's and ours.

# LESSON 5
Ruth 2:14-23

## OPENING QUESTION
Tell of a time you invited others to your home for a meal, and something either funny, embarrassing or delightful happened.

## ACCEPTANCE (v. 14)
1. What does it mean when you invite someone to your home for a meal? What are your intentions and your hopes?

2. Boaz served Ruth bread, wine and roasted grain. Describe what else might have occurred as the workers had their meal.

3. The law shuts out, but grace invites in. Boaz, in sharing the bread and wine with Ruth, exemplified such grace. God's grace to us is the Cross which is proclaimed in the Lord's supper - Holy Communion. What was it Boaz was proclaiming to Ruth and his workers when he invited her to eat?
We find God's hospitality in communion

Share what Holy Communion means to you.

4. Ruth ate all she wanted and had some left over. We have discussed how Jesus, in John 6, feeds the 5000 providing more than enough. Why do you think Jesus multiplied more bread than necessary to feed the 5000?

39

5. Why do you think Boaz gave Ruth more than she could possibly eat?

6. What does this tell us about the character of Boaz and also the character of Christ?

## WORKING TOGETHER (vs. 15-16)

1. Boaz instructs his men to not "embarrass" Ruth nor "rebuke" her. What does Boaz mean by this?

2. Read John 4:36-38. How does this scripture support these verses in Ruth?

## ABUNDANCE and SHARING (vs. 17-18)

1. Ruth gleaned an ephah in one day. This is approximately ½ month's wages. What is the Lord showing Ruth? *What can we learn from that - what do we make of this?*

2. Read James 2:14-18. Boaz is a James 2:14-18 man in his treatment of others. Actions toward others are very important. Tell of a time someone's actions toward you showed unusual love.

3. Ruth shares her blessing with Naomi. Name two ways you are currently being blessed and how you might in turn bless others with that blessing.

## HOPE (vs. 19-20)

1. Hope comes alive in Naomi when she realizes the good intentions of Boaz, a kinsman-redeemer. We hear her rejoice over this. What things about God's character causes you to rejoice at this time in your life?

## PROTECTION & PROVISION (vs. 21-23)

1. Ruth will be protected (covered) in Boaz's fields. Sometimes we stray from God's covering. Share a time you have taken yourself out of God's covering or you've seen someone else do so. What happened?

2. Ruth is told to "stay close." She stays close to the servant girls and she stays close to Naomi. In this we are seeing closeness in society and closeness in family. Keeping close is for blessing. What can you do to increase closeness in your family? In society?

## CLOSING

Look over what we have thus far covered in the book of Ruth. Can you see evidence that Boaz is attracted to Ruth? What are these evidences?

## WHAT DID YOU LEARN?

# LESSON 6

# RUTH 3:1-9

# Preparation of the Bride

**Access to the Throne**

## Lesson 6 Introduction

In Lesson 6, hope has been ignited in Naomi. Knowing Jewish law, she shares with Ruth her plan: Ruth is to go to the threshing floor and propose marriage to Boaz.... in the Jewish manner, of course. What boldness and courage this will require on Ruth's part.

Let's look at Ruth, who is symbolic of the Church, the Bride of Christ, as she prepares herself for Boaz. Let's look deep into why she was able do such a bold thing and consider how we in like manner, can also boldly approach the throne of God.

# LESSON 6
## Ruth 3:1-9

**OPENING QUESTION**

If you are married, share how you and your husband got engaged. Who asked who and how it was done? If you are unmarried, how is it you would like to be proposed to when the time comes?

**A PLAN (vs. 1-2)**

Remember Jeremiah 29:11 where it says that God has a plan for you, to prosper you and give you a future? Naomi, God's instrument for a higher plan, not only has a plan but the plan is to be carried out right now, tonight!

1. If you were Ruth, how might you have reacted to this idea of Naomi's?

2. The Jewish law of kinsman-redeemer was not an obligation but a right. Therefore, Boaz could reject or accept his position of kinsman-redeemer. What was Naomi thinking? Was she confident or taking a chance with Boaz's acceptance? Why do you think this?

**PREPARATION (vs. 3-4)**

1. Just as a bride is to prepare for her bridegroom, Naomi instructs Ruth to do three things before going to the threshing floor. What are they?


   What was the purpose in doing these three things? (Eph 5:26 might be a clue).


2. Read Titus 3:5 and Ephesians 5:26. What are some facts about us being washed through Christ?


3. Ruth anointed herself with perfume. II Cor. 2:14-16 says, "But thanks be to God who always leads us in triumphal procession in Christ and through us spreads everywhere the fragrance of the knowledge of Him. For we are to God the aroma of Christ among those who are being saved and those who are perishing. To one we are the smell of death; to the other the fragrance of life."

   Metaphorically, what aroma was Ruth spreading to Boaz that night?


   You are an aroma of Christ to God. How do we emit that fragrance to the world?

4. Ruth was to put on her best clothes. The church in the end times is given fine linen, bright and clean, to wear. Look up the following scripture and write down what the fine linen of the saints symbolizes.

Rev. 19:7-8 Fine linen stands for _____

5. Read James 2:24-25. What was Ruth's righteous act of faith? What was Rahab's? (Rahab was Boaz's mother, by the way).

6. II Timothy 2:20-21 talks of being ordinary vessels but cleansed to be used for noble purposes. Apply this to Ruth's story and Rahab's What can we say about Ruth and the mother of Boaz (Rahab)?

7. How about you? In what ways can you see God changing you into a noble vessel for Him? Is he convicting you to change anything or to take up something new?

## APPROPRIATING GOD'S WORD (vs. 5-9)

1. Ruth was told to lie down at Boaz's feet and uncover them. This was a Jewish tradition. It was an invitation to Boaz for marriage and a request for his protection. His kinsman-redeemer position is being appealed to. Ruth approaches Boaz, rather than Boaz approaching Ruth. Why do you think it was this way?

2. James 4:2 tells us "We have not because we ask not." Why is it we have to ask for some things? (prayer is asking). What is God after?

3. If there is a willing relative, the kinsman-redeemer law will provide for Ruth and Naomi and also carry on the family line of Elimelech. Ruth met the conditions of this law by being a widow of a Jew, but would Boaz be willing? For us, Christ had a choice also. He was not forced to die on the cross for us and redeem us but He could if He chose to. (You might want to read the passages of Jesus' prayers in the Garden of Gethsemane - Matt. 26:36-46 - that occurred right before the crucifixion). If Boaz agrees to marry Ruth, he will be granting that his inheritance will go to the family of Elimilech. Christ, agreeing to redeem us, gives us an inheritance. What are your thoughts on the willingness of Boaz, then Christ, to do this?

4. Hebrews 4:16 says, "let us then approach the throne of grace with confidence, so that we may receive mercy and find grace to help us in our time of need." A throne of GRACE! What is your understanding of grace? Use a dictionary or scriptures to discover what grace is and put a definition here in your own words:

5. Ruth humbly came to the feet of Boaz in submission, but boldly she was requesting redemption. At the feet of the cross, we come submitting to God and asking for redemption. Boaz covered Ruth with the corner of his garment; Christ covers us with His blood.

Below are some thoughts about Ruth submitting to Boaz and Boaz protecting Ruth. In the second section, write down your thoughts regarding submitting to Christ and Christ protecting you.

Ruth and Boaz:
  Submission –Ruth submits to Boaz, to be called by his name, to come under his rule, to share the marriage bed.

  Protection- Boaz protects Ruth by securing her future and providing for her needs.

  You and Christ
  Submission – To submit to Christ is to

  Protection – Christ protects us in that He


**DEEPER**
1. Appropriating God's word is much like Ruth appropriating the law of kinsman-redeemer; she merely laid it down before Boaz. Psalm 145:13 tells us "The Lord is faithful to all His promises and loving toward all He has made." What does this tell you about the probability of God acting on His promises when we present them to him?


2. Some promises are conditional (have a pre-requisite or a requirement). Some are not. Read the promises below, then write down the promise as you see it, followed by the condition, if there is one. The first one is done for you.

   **Psalm 25:9** He guides the humble in what is right and teaches them his way.

   The Promise:  He will guide me and teach me his ways.
   The Condition: To be humble. Humble, we listen and do.

49

**Matthew 6:33** But seek first his kingdom and his righteousness, and all these things (food, clothing, etc.) will be given to you as well.

The Promise:

The Condition:

**Isaiah 43:1-2** Fear not, for I have redeemed you. When you pass through the waters I will be with you; and when you pass though the rivers, they will not sweep over you. When you walk through the fire, you will not be burned; the flames will not set you ablaze.

The Promises:

The Condition:

**James 4:8** Come near to God and he will come near to you.

The Promise:

The Condition:

**Romans 8:28** All things God works for the good of those who love him, who have been called according to his purpose.

The Promise:

The Condition:

## CLOSING

1. Ruth was first a servant to Boaz, then she became a friend (they ate together). Finally, she makes a request to be his wife. All of these are right relationships we can have with the Lord as well. Describe these three relationships *between Boaz and Ruth* from the angle of our relationship with Christ.

A servant:

A friend:


A wife/husband:


2. Based on your answers, what is the most exciting part about having a bride/bridegroom relationship with the Lord?


**PERSONAL THOUGHT:**
Ruth approached Boaz with humility (a servant) and with courage (boldness). Is there a promise (from His word) the Lord wants you to take to His feet? (Appropriate it; speak it and come to believe it for you personally). What is it?


**WHAT DID YOU LEARN?**

# LESSON 7

# Ruth 3:10-18

# TEST OF FAITH

**God is with me. I shall not be afraid!**

## Lesson 7 Introduction

Boaz's response to Ruth's request to be her kinsman-redeemer is hopeful, but probably not exactly what Ruth was wanting to hear. Boaz acknowledges there is another and closer relative who is first in line to fulfill the kinsman-redeemer role. Who is this person who could now become Ruth's new husband? Ruth had stepped out in faith, boldly approached the feet of Boaz, and now findes her future in the hands of a stranger, not Boaz. Or is it?

Ruth has a long night ahead of her. How is her faith going to hold up? Is her new God to be trusted or not? These are things Ruth must decide.

There are questions for us in Lesson 7. Who is this God we claim to trust in? Do we, without a doubt, know that He is a good God? What are His promises and can we stand on them?

## LESSON 7
Ruth 3:10-18

**OPENING QUESTION**
We have all seen a time when a small child is expected to take a leap into his daddy's arms and the child hesitates, wondering, "Will Daddy really catch me?" Maybe it is that first lunge into a swimming pool. It looks frightening, but there is your Papa or Momma saying they will catch you. Can you trust them? Are they going to do what they say they will do? Share a time you had to trust God and it was hard.

**BOAZ'S RESPONSE (vs. 10-11)**
1. Much is revealed in verses 10 and 11 and further on about the charcter of Ruth and Boaz. What do you see regarding:
   Ruth's character:

   Boaz's character:

2. Why do you think Boaz told Ruth "Do not be afraid?

3. I John 4:18 says, "There is no fear in love, but perfect love casts out fear because fear has to do with punishment. The one who fears is not made perfect in love." Apply this to Boaz telling Ruth to not be afraid. What does it mean?

4. How does it make you feel to know that God is for you?

## THE TEST (vs. 12-13)

1. Naomi had chosen Boaz because he had already shown himself willing to be a protector. But now we are told there is another who is a closer relative than Boaz, and he has the first right of kinsman-redeemer. Ruth is told to stay the night and sleep 'til morning. How could she sleep! If you were Ruth, what would you now be thinking?

2. Obligation or love? If obligation was all Boaz felt, how might he have responded to Ruth, in light of the fact that there was this other relative?

3. Boaz would follow the Jewish course of law and talk with the relative who is first in line to be kinsman-redeemer. Boaz's words: "If he wants to redeem, good, let him redeem," are not real comforting words for Ruth. Does it mean he doesn't "care" which way it goes? If not that, then what is he really saying?

4. Let's look at the unnamed redeemer as the "law" and Boaz as "grace" or "love." How is the other redeemer, who has no relationship with Ruth, like the law?

5. "As surely as the Lord lives, I will do it." This is the oath, Boaz speaks to Ruth regarding her redemption. How do you picture Boaz when he speaks this? Happy? Peaceful? Excited? Somber? Unfeeling? Explain.

6. Numbers 23:19 says that God does not lie but his promises he fulfills. We *say* we believe that God stands by His Word, but do we really believe that? Are there any of His promises you struggle with believing? (i.e. He loves you unconditionally; He has a purpose for your life etc.). Which one?

7. "Lie down until morning," Boaz says. Read I Peter 1:13 then re-word Boaz's comment to Ruth according to this scripture.

## ENCOURAGEMENT (vs. 14-15)

1. Boaz's instructions in verse 14 show us his concern for what?

2. Ruth, going to the threshing floor and spending the night there, could be misunderstood. On the otherhand, it could be considered a very holy moment like when you or I might bow at God's feet in prayer and supplication. At the feet of Jesus birthing can occur - answered prayers, new found peace, hearing him speak into a situation. Take time to be quiet before the Lord and benefit being at His feet. Sense the moment is holy. Is there anything you would care to share or make note of here? About Ruth or yourself?

3. Romans 10:11 says, "Anyone who trusts in him will never be put to shame." At this point in the story we could say Ruth's future is

in limbo. Will it go the way of the law (the unnamed kinsman-redeemer) or the way of love and grace (Boaz)? Boaz said to her "Do not be afraid." Jesus says to us "If you trust in me, you will not be put to shame." What does it mean to "not be put to shame?" What does it have to do with trusting?

4. Boaz put barley into Ruth's shawl as a seal of his promise. Read the scripture below and discover how God gave us His seal.

*And you also were included in Christ when you heard the message of truth, the gospel of your salvation. When you believed, you were marked in him with a seal, the promised Holy Spirit, who is a deposit guaranteeing our inheritance until the redemption of those who are God's possession—to the praise of his glory.* Ephesians 1:13-14

What was the blessing from the seal of barley for Ruth?

How does the Holy Spirit bless us, serving as a seal?

Explain the parallel.

## NAOMI'S WISDOM (vs. 16-18)
1. Naomi says, "wait." The Hebrew word used is also used for "sit." What is Naomi communicating?

## DEEPER
Christ upon the cross (pre- resurrection) may have caused doubt in many of His followers. Jesus was supposed to be king and here he was being crucified. At this point, the disciples may have been in doubt about their own future. Ruth is being tested much like they were. Boaz

58

appeared to be that perfect man who would redeem her and protect her But now, she is informed that there is this other relative. (Much like Satan had ownership of us before the Cross). Sometimes things are the darkest before the light finally comes forth. The death of our Christ appeared to be so very dark, but then the glorious resurrection occurred. Do you have a story about your darkest hour and the light that came through?

**CLOSING**
I Thessalonians 5:11 says "Therefore, encourage one another, and build up one another." Naomi was doing this with Ruth, passing on her faith for this situation. Let's now encourage one another. For a moment be still and listen to the Holy Spirit and ask him to give you a word of encouragement or a scripture to encourage someone in your bible study. What is that word He is giving you?

**WHAT DID YOU LEARN?**

# LESSON 8

# Ruth 4: 1-8

# THE CONTRACT

**A Covenant of Love**

Lesson 8 Introduction

We know God's word is true and that what he says He will do, He will.

Boaz, too, is true to his word and promise. Just as he said he would, Boaz, that very morning goes to the town gate to settle the issue with the other kinsman-redeemer (the law).

A contract is made, a legal deal…. And Ruth's redemption is settled. This wonderful contract is not about obligation but it is about love, just like the new covenant given us by Christ is all about love!

Prepare for Lesson 8 with these verses.
Circle key words and jot down thoughts.

Matthew 5:17 *Do you think I came to abolish the Law or the Prophets; I have not come to abolish them but to fulfill them.*

Romans 7:4 *Through the body of Christ we die to the law so we would bear fruit to God.*

Romans 8:3 *For what the law was powerless to do in that it was weakened by the sinful nature, God did by sending his own son in the likeness of sinful man to be a sin offering.*

Romans 13:8 *Let no debt remain outstanding, except the continuing debt to love one another for he who loves his fellowman has fulfilled the law.*

II Corinthians 5:14-15 *For Christ's love compels us, because we are convinced that one died for all and therefore all died. And he died for all that those who live should no longer live for themselves, but for him who died for them and was raised again.*

Galatians 3:25 *Now that faith has come, we are no longer under the supervision* (judgment) *of the law.*

# LESSON 8
## Ruth 4:1-8

---

**OPENING QUESTIONS**
Tell your study group of any domestic task (chore), or other family obligation, that you grow weary of doing. What is it and why is it burdensome?

If there are no burdensome tasks in your life, please share your secret with us!

**MEETING WITH THE UNNAMED RELATIVE  (vs. 1-2)**
1. Looking at this Jewish custom (law) of the kinsman-redeemer, do you see it as a good or flawed law and why?

2. We can assume Boaz felt this to be *urgent* business for he did not put it off. Instead, he set out that very morning. Why do you think he treated it so urgently?

3. Boaz called the unnamed relative "friend." Is it possible for us to look at the law, which shows us our shortcomings and points out sin, as a friend also? Why? (Read Galatians 3:24. and find what the purpose of God's law is.)

**DIPLOMACY (vs. 3-4)**
1. What is the purpose/goal of being diplomatic?

2. Boaz, being diplomatic, gives only half the facts of the contract at the start: that there is an opportunity to buy some land and it is (he unnamed relative's opportunity first. Boaz does not mention the

63

obligation of marriage to Ruth at this point if the man chooses to redeem the land. Why did Boaz do it this way?

## THE SMALL PRINT (vs. 5-6)

1. Boaz reveals the rest of the contract. (The small print we would say). Look specifically at verse 5. What are the two issues which cause this unnamed relative's ears to perk up?

2. The unnamed kinsman-redeemer, who before said yes, now says he CANNOT redeem because he would endanger his own estate. One way this would happen is if he and Ruth had only one heir (child); all he had would go to that child. Pretend you are this relative. In your own words, how would you explain to your best friend why you don't want to endanger your estate. (See notes on redemption in the Appendix).

   Your statement might begin like this. . . .

   "I had an opportunity today to redeem the land of Naomi, Elimilech's widow. I almost jumped to do this, except for the fact

   _____

   _____

   _____

   _____

   _____

   _____

3. Just like the law (Galatians 3:24) serves a purpose, so this relative serves a purpose. What is his purpose and what is the message to us?

4. Boaz will gladly redeem Ruth and the land (see Ruth 3:11) though the risks are the same for him as for the other relative. He will pay the FULL price, purchase the land AND marry Ruth even though his name *may* not be carried on in Israel and another man's (Elimilech's) will. Why would any Jew do this and risk his name being blotted out?

## The LAW VS CHRIST

1. The law says, "I *canno*t redeem you because I am unable to get rid of your baggage."

   Christ says, "I *can* redeem you because I willing to sacrifice to make you righteous. I will be your righteousness by dying."

   We have opportunity to die every day for family, friends, acquaintances and strangers. How is that going for you? To die, or serve at a cost, for others?

   - o   I just don't see many opportunities.
   - o   I realize I let many opportunities go.
   - o   I can sacrifice for my family but not for a stranger.
   - o   I can sacrifice for family even a stranger, but an evil person… no.
   - o   I have learned the blessing of dying at every opportunity the Lord presents to me for any one - family, friend, stranger, enemy.

   Why is it so hard for us? Your thoughts on all of this:

2. Boaz knew the other redeemer would not redeem Ruth much like God knew the law could not save us. Like Ruth needed Boaz for redemption, we need Christ for ours.
   How would you explain the need for redemption to an unbeliever?

   How would you explain *your* Redeemer to an unbeliever?

3. God so loved the world that he gave his only son that whosoever believes in him shall not perish but have eternal life. (John 3:16). Finish the sentence below using John 3:16 as your base:

   Boaz so loved Ruth that he . . .

## THE CONTRACT IS SEALED (vs. 7-8)

The passing of the sandal was a forfeiting of the relative's right to redeem the property and widow. It is now public record that Boaz accepted this right and will marry Ruth. Boaz redeemed both the land and Ruth, not by force or out of obligation, but by his own will and out of love. This is what Ruth will remember, not the unnamed relative's refusal, but Boaz's *willingness* and desire to redeem her.

1.  If the unnamed relative (the law) had agreed to marry Ruth, what pressures might he have put on her? What pressures does the law put on us?


2.  We could say Christ accepted the sandal from the law, agreeing to go to the Cross. Jesus said, "I lay down my life for the sheep" (John 10:15), and "I lay it down on my own accord." (John 10:18).

    What does the cross say to you after studying this portion of Ruth?


3.  Col. 2:13-15 describes the Christians rebirth. It also tells us the wonderful works of the Cross. List them here:

    God made me _____.
    He _____ all my _____.
    He canceled _____.
    He also _____ it to the cross.
    He _____ the powers and authorities.
    He _____ over the powers and
    authorities as well!

    (Note: powers and authorities are the forces of the demonic).

4. What do we no longer have to fear?


5. What does Ruth no longer have to fear?

## DEEPER

The unnamed kinsman was unwilling to risk his inheritance for a stranger. Romans 5:7 says "Very rarely will anyone die for a righteous man, though for a good man someone might possibly dare to die. But God demonstrates his own love for us in this: while we were still sinners (a Moabite), Christ died for us."

Love enables us to die for another. Who in your family can you begin to honor with a new attitude of sacrificial love toward them?

How are you going to do this?

## WHAT DID YOU LEARN?

# LESSON 9

# Ruth 4:9-12

# BEYOND SELF

**It Is Not About Me!**

Lesson 9 Introduction

As the story of Ruth has progressed, it has become evident that much
of God's truths can be learned in this small book of the Old
Testamnent. Also, as we study Ruth we see that the characters serve
as representations to help us understand God's love for us.

Naomi represents the church
Ruth represents the individual believer
Boaz represents the Christ
Orpah represents those who reject the faith, resisting love
The unnamed relative represents the law
The town records represent the Book of Life!!

In Lesson 9 a marriage has been announced and blessings are being
spoken. As we look at the blessings, we see they do not just concern
one family nor just one man and one woman; they involve all of Israel.
What does this say to us? Do we consider ourselves part of a whole?

Open your heart in Lesson 9 and let God put good things into it!

# LESSON 9
## Ruth 4:9-12

**OPENING QUESTION**

Is there an heirloom in your family you can tell us about? Whose was it and why is it special to you? Why do we keep heirlooms?

**PUBLIC PROCLAMATION (vs. 9-10)**

1. Boaz *proclaims* in the hearing of all, two things. What are they and why does he proclaim them so publicly?

2. What is the result of Boaz's buying and acquiring? Who will be affected besides Boaz, Ruth, Naomi?

3. If the name of the dead is not maintained what happens?

4. We see in Ruth that from generation to generation family kept family names going, kept them in the "town records." What is our responsibility to our descendents in light of God's records of who belong to Him? (See Deuteronomy 7:9).

**THE BOOK OF LIFE**

1. When we are born again (redeemed), our name goes into God's Book of Life. The heavenly witnesses rejoice in our salvation. What is it we are now inheriting because our names are in His book? (Matthew 19:29).

2. If Boaz can maintain Mahlon's name for all time, consider how much more Christ can maintain your name in the Book of Life. Boaz keeps a family name alive, to be remembered forever in Israel. What about your name being forever in the Book of Life?

   Read Psalm 111:5b. What does it say about God's covenant with us?

   Read Psalm 37:22-24. What is holding you up?

3. We see the town people very happy about Ruth and Boaz. Why are they just as happy as Naomi and Ruth?

4. Do *you* share community joy in the body of Christ? Share with us a story of someone's moment of salvation that you greatly rejoiced in. Describe your reaction and emotions.

5. Ruth and Naomi now had assurance that the family name would remain in the records. If a believer does not have this assurance, but instead they doubt their salvation, what can we tell them? How can we minister to them?

## BLESSINGS (vs. 11-12)

The elders at the gate are not only witnesses to the kinsmen-redeemer transaction, but they are also givers of blessings to Boaz and Ruth. There are three blessings given.

## THE FIRST BLESSING

1. What is the first blessing spoken over Boaz and Ruth by the elders and those at the gate?

2. Rachel and Leah built up the house of Israel. (Exodus 1:1-5). Ruth, as well, is part of building up the house of Israel through here descentent David, and later through the Messiah, Jesus the Christ. For the elders to give such a blessing tells us what about these people?

3. How can we be part of the building up of the church?

## THE SECOND BLESSING

1. What is the 2nd blessing spoken by the elders?

2. Did this come to pass? What is Boaz remembered for?

3. What does it mean for us to have good standing with God or with one another in the church?

## THE THIRD BLESSING

1. What is the 3rd blessing?

2. Tamar was a recipient of the kinsman-redeemer law, bearing twins to Judah. When this blessing is spoken to Boaz and Ruth, who else are the people thinking and what is their concern?

3. Both Perez and David both brought rest to the people of Israel. Consider your rest coming from your assurance of salvation. How does this assurance give you rest?

## APPLICATION

1. What are the blessings you would want (or have wanted) for your children when they marry?

2. Compare your blessings for your children with the three blessings pronounced over Boaz and Ruth. How do yours differ?

3. In hindsight (or foresight), what blessing would you have liked prayed over you and your husband when you married? Or over you and your future husband?

## BEYOND OUR SELF

Boaz and Ruth sacrificed for Naomi bringing rest to her life. David conquered the enemies of Israel bringing rest to the nation. Jesus brings us rest and will bring us our final rest. He selflessly died for all the world.

1. If we look beyond our self, we can benefit and bless others.

   Who were the beneficiaries of Boaz and Ruth? _____
   Who were the beneficiaries of David? _____
   Who are the beneficiaries of the Messiah? _____

2. We are just one small part of a whole. But one person can do a lot
   as we see above, especially if they are yielded to God. You *can* be
   instrumental in building up Jerusalem (the Body of Christ, the
   Church). You *can* be instrumental in bringing God's rest and
   peace to someone else.

   Here are some ways you can be used by God for the Kingdom.
   Add some of your own.

   - Be a spokesman for God - share the gospel.
   - Be a light of his love to a hurting individual.
   - Be someone who will pray for others.
   - Be someone who will encourage others.
   - (other)_____
   - (other)_____

3. We can have "people eyes" to see a need and then minister to it.
   Why did these people in Bethlehem have eyes for all their people?

Pray for one another this week that you would
become more available to God in whatever way
He wants to use you.

….Let your heart grow…..expand out ….for others.

**WHAT DID YOU LEARN?**

# LESSON 10

# RUTH 4:13-22

# FRUITFULNESS

Sowing to the Eternal!

Lesson 10 Introduction

As the Book of Ruth concludes, the story's focus returns to Naomi. Naomi, who once was empty, now is made full.

We look at a family tree, Perez's, which includes Boaz, Obed, and David the king who brought Israel from unrest to rest. (In Matthew Chapter 1 we find more of the genealogy line where it leads to Jesus, the Messiah). The family tree yet continues. We, believers in Christ, are in that tree. We are children of God through Jesus Christ. So, way back to the story of Ruth, we were on God's mind.

## LESSON 10
### Ruth 4:13-22

**OPENING QUESTION**

When someone has a bountiful garden or a high-producing fruit tree, they often share it's harvest with others. Tell of a time you were blessed by someone else's bounty, what it was and what it meant to you that they shared it, of all people, with you.

**FRUITFULNESS IN MARRIAGE (v. 13)**

1. A marriage. A conception. A son. What was God's part in this scenario in Ruth? Why is it so amazing?

2. Read John 15:16. What does it say about you?

3 The rest of John 15 talks about abiding (dwelling) in the vine (Christ). The more we abide, the more fruit we will bear. (types of fruit in this passage are answered prayer, godly character and joy.) Consider natural fruit and the various ways they are enjoyed by us? What is it we like about fruit?

4. Now consider spiritual fruit. Is there any similarity in how spiritual fruit is enjoyed by the members of the Church?

**FRUITFULNESS Beyond the Marriage (vs. 14-15)**

1. "Blessed is the Lord" the women say. Very simply, what are the women doing by saying this?

2.  Name someone you consider famous. Why are they famous? If you were related to them, how might that affect how other people think of you or relate to you?

3.  If Obed is famous because he is "related" to the much-loved King David, and he is also related to Jesus Christ, whom we are also related to, then aren't we also famous? In light of this, how might we pray for the success and future of our children? Who is the one we want them related to above all others?

4.  Naomi's friends are specific in stating how this baby is to be a blessing to Naomi. They refer to him as a "restorer of _____ and a sustainer _____. What might these mean to Naomi?

5.  Read I Peter 5:10. In this passage, what is the result of being restored?

6.  Look at these other verses on being restored. Fill in the blanks, as you answer, "What is it that is being restored?"

    Ps 51:12 Restore to me the _____ of your salvation
    Ps 23:3 He restores my _____

7.  Why would our God do this for us?

8. Using a dictionary, write down the definition of "sustain." Now read Psalm 55:22 and Hebrews 1:3 and answer: How are we sustained?

9. Personalize the truth of God's sustaining us by filling in the blanks. (example: When I give the Lord my worries, he will bear them.)

   When I give the Lord my _____ he will _____
   _____.

   His powerful _____ will _____
   me.

10. Ruth is given a great compliment (v. 15) in a day when men and sons were highly valued over women and daughters. Complete the following thought:

    JESUS is better to me than

    _____          _____
    a number            (husband(s), friend(s), teacher(s), etc.)

11. What does completing that sentence make you realize?

**FRUITFULNESS for ALL (vs. 16-17)**
1. Because the child of Ruth and Boaz will be known as the son of Elimilech and Naomi, his birth is the culmination of joy for Naomi. But what of Ruth? What might we guess is going on with her? Is this hard for her or easy? Why or why not?

2. It is the women who give Obed his name. What do you think about that? What does this say about the character of Boaz and Ruth?

3. Obed (or Obadiah) means servant of God. Why do you think they chose that name?

4. If you were the one to name this baby with a Hebrew name, what would be it's meaning?

## TWO FAMILY TREES (vs. 18-22)

1. Though Obed was considered the son of Elimilech in the town records, here in the genealogy he is referred to as the son of Boaz. We can conclude then that Obed was considered the son of Naomi and Elimilech only for the purpose of _____.
But he is really the son of _____.

2. Fill in the blanks:
Jesus is the son of J_____ and M_____ of Bethlehem.
Jesus is the Son of G_____.

For what purpose was Jesus born of man similar to Obed's purpose?

3. All that we have, we are to consider belonging to God. With that attitude, what might be the meaning of the name you give your own child?
_____ of God.

## YOUR GENEALOGY:

1. If you did a study of your ancestors, what information about them would bless you the most?

2. The following is for your own private reflection. In this condensed
   version of a family tree, fill in the names of your earthly family on
   the left. On the right put the name of those whom you know have
   (or did have) a relationship with Jesus Christ.

| Your Earthly Family | The Holy Family |
|---|---|
| A grandfather or grandmother | Child of God? |
| Your father (or mother) | Child of God? |
| Your name | Child of God? |
| One of your children | Child of God? |
| A grandchild | Child of God? |

How can *you* sow to the eternal through family?

## APPLICATION

God gives us gifts for giving and blessing others. Obed was a gift
given away. Jesus was a gift given away. (John 3:16). Boaz and Ruth
are givers. We too are to give (share) gifts, especially spiritual gifts.
As you look up these verses, consider that you have a call to give and
bless within the church and to the world. Please list the gifts from I
Corinthians 12:7-11.

1. The 9 spiritual gifts listed are:

_____  _____  _____
_____  _____  _____
_____  _____  _____

83

In verse 7 we are told these gifts are for the common good. What does that mean?

2. Read I Corinthians 12:27-31. Where are these gifts to be used (verse 28)?

3. I Corinthians 13:1 says "Follow the way of love and eagerly desire spiritual gifts, especially the gift of prophecy." How would you "eagerly" desire spiritual gifts and why would you do so?

4. Read Romans 12:5-8 and list the seven gifts:

   _____  _____  _____
   _____  _____  _____
   _____

   The phrase "let him" is repeated and repeated! Why would this be repeated? What is the emphasis?

5. Which of the above gifts would you consider asking God for and why?

**CLOSING**
Do one of the following:
1. Share a time that someone blessed you through their spiritual gift.

2. Share a time the Lord restored your soul with the Word of God.

**WHAT DID YOU LEARN?**

# WHAT I REAPED FROM THIS STUDY
Having completed this study of The Book of Ruth, I can say that it......

- o Changed me.
  How?


- o Awakened something new in me.
  What?


- o Made me realize how much God loves me. How?


- o Helped me understand the character of God more clearly.
  Specifically -


- o Other:

## FOOTNOTES

Background Information
1 – Internet webpage: http://toriavey.com/what-is-shavuot3

2 – Internet webpage,
http://www.myjewishlearning.com/article/why-do-we-read-the-book-of-ruth-on-shavuot/ Excerpted with permission from Every Person's Guide to Shavuot (Jason Aronson, Inc).

3 - The NIV Study Bible New International Version, 1985, Introduction notes to Ruth, 363.

4 - New Bible Commentary, 21st Century Edition, 1994, Inter-Varsity Press, p. 287.

Lesson 1
1 - New Bible Commentary, 21st Century Edition, 1994, Inter-Varsity Press, p. 289.

# APPENDIX

# LESSON HELPS FOR GROUP LEADER
Answers given to questions in this Help Section are not exhaustive answers. Members of your Bible study will have other wonderful answers to contribute.

## LESSON 1
This was a time of Israel's apostasy characterized by unbelief, not following God, moral degradation and foreign oppression.

### LEAVING
- Bethlehem, where Jesus was born, means *House of Bread*. It was so named because it was an extremely fertile land.
- The Moabites were idolaters. Their god was Chemosh who was worshiped by child sacrifice.

Question 1: Possible pros: food, work, adventure. Possible cons: leaving behind family and friends, risking how the Moabites will receive them, living with a "different" people, no synagogue available.
Question 2: It might be that his faith and his people the Jews were not his first priority, but feeding his family was. It might be that he was disappointed in God, who was not providing for them as expected.
Question 3: We will either see Elimelech, the leader of his family, as weak or wise. We will see him either regretful or not. But selection c is definitely true.
Question 4: They left not just a place, but family, friends, their history, their fellowship in the synagogue and support from others. They would be starting over with all these.

Another point to consider is that maybe God was in this more than realized. Possibly, this family's move was for the purpose of one day bringing Ruth to Bethlehem where she would meet Boaz.

### PRESSURE
Genesis 19 tells the story of Lot and the beginning of the Moabites.

Question 1: To name their child *God is King* would imply Elimelech's parents had both faith and hope. Possibly, this was descriptive of their whole generation. It was not that *God is our Provider*, or *God is Mighty* that they named their son, but *God is King* – they considered themselves a nation and God was their supreme and divine King.

Question 2: The names of Elimelech's two sons reveal there was great struggle in having children, that they went through trials and many sicknesses to have even two sons. Their years in Bethlehem were hard.

Question 3: It appears possibly Elimelech died right off. Maybe he was sickly when they left Bethlehem or soon after. We don't know. But He died and Naomi and her sons remained in Moab. This requires the bible study participants to use their imagination and write some fiction. The question to ask is, why had they not returned to Bethlehem yet. Was it finances? Did the sons not want to leave Moab? All is speculation.

Question 4: Leaving Bethlehem for economic gain, we might assume Elimelech was struggling with God and faith. Because they were not blessed in Moab, it might have been out of the will of God. Or. Maybe not. But we know this, most of Bethlehem stayed in Bethlehem as no mention of others leaving is mentioned.

Question 5: If no one wants to share their personal experiences, the group can discuss the emptying that occurs when we lose a loved one, lose a job, go through divorce or struggle with anger and disappointment with God.

DECISION TO RETURN

Question 1: Naomi heard the famine was over and God was again blessing His people. Naomi was hopeful and her faith stirred. (Another twist you might add to this question is how we respond when we hear of a revival happening somewhere – an outbreak of God. Are our hearts pricked or not?)

Question 2: Some are drawn to God because He is a God of love, gives us peace, joy and family. Others may be drawn because they are ridden with guilt and need to know His forgiveness. Any of God's attributes can draw us to Him. Some are drawn hearing of a personal relationship with God is possible. Enjoy the individual testimonies in your group.

Question 3: Naomi's heart has always been in Bethlehem and Moab was never home.

Question 4: What of your faith do you treasure the most? What would cause you to swim oceans or cross mountains in order to return to it? Possible answers: His presence. His Word. His comfort.

Question 5: Do we think of Naomi as strong, revived, inspired? No wrong answers to this question.

Question 6: The discussion can go many places with this question. Points to be considered:
- What leaving requires of us
- The place we are – do we cling to anything and shouldn't? Or are we at a place it feels right to leave?
- What was Naomi's heart feeling?
- Roads – what is our way back to God?
- What do we return to when we return to God?

Question 7: Was Naomi looking forward and not back? What is the advantage of looking forward when we are returning to God. She was leaving behind the graves of her husband and son. How would that feel?

REPENTANCE

Question 1: Repentance is a turning. Turning away from sin and returning to a right place with God. Both the heart and our actions change when we repent.

Question 2: Naomi's return might be considered repentance because she is now wanting to fully embrace God's people, God's land and God's ways. She is returning to the fold.

Consider bringing these points into your discussion.
- If you will repent, I will restore you. (Jer. 15:19)
- Repent and do the things you did at first. (Rev. 2:5)
- Naomi's returning showed she was hungry for God and the people of God. (Mt. 5:6)
- God rewards those who seek Him will all their heart. (Heb. 11:6)

CLOSING

Question 1: The difference? One is going to the unknown and the other to the known. One was leaving behind and the other is picking back up.

## LESSON 2
### OPTIONS
Question 1: Naomi asks that the God of Israel would bless her daughters-in-law (reciprocate their goodness) and provide them with new husbands.

Question 2: Though she was emptied, Naomi still knows there is goodness from the Lord.

Question 3: They were both good women. They loved their husbands and Naomi.

Question 4: She might have entreated them harder to come with her, promising good things in Israel.

Question 5: Maybe Naomi respected their faith and did not press the issue of faith in Jehovah. This might be because she was struggling with her faith. Another possibility is the girls were keen on their Moab god and were not interested in their husbands' God.

### WISDOM OF THE WORLD – PULL OF REASONING
Question 1: Naomi's reasons are due to the custom of Levitical marriage which states a widow is not to marry outside the family. Naomi was releasing the younger women from this. Right or wrong, Naomi was kind.

Question 2: Naomi was not hopeful of good things at this point. Her lack of hope was based on past experience.

Question 4: (Genesis) Eve, using her own reasoning, led to her downfall. Naomi was applying her own reasoning in telling the girls to remain in Moab. (Proverbs) Ruth trusted in the pull of her heart, which was actually God. She refused the reasoning Naomi gave her. (1 Corinthians) To Orpah, it may have looked foolish for Ruth to go with Naomi but it wasn't foolishness, but life.

### TWO DIFFERENT DECISIONS
Question 1: Orpah's reasons for staying might have been she believed there was no hope in Israel for her and she wanted to live again. Ruth's reasons for going with Naomi? Her self did not matter, only Naomi.

Question 2: Her people and her gods.

Question 3: Possibly, Ruth had for a long time found the God of Israel appealing. Not so with Oprah. There can be many other reasons.

Question 4: Pull from all any of these comments about choosing true life – life in God:

- Naomi lost her life in Moab in order to find it again in her return to Bethlehem.
- Orpah felt she was choosing life and a future, but it was a temporal promise… she was settling for life only on this earth. Choosing life in Moab, she lost life in Bethlehem.
- Ruth was choosing to give up her life for Naomi and Naomi's God. She received life.
- To go with Naomi was foolishness to Orpah, but to Ruth it was life and joy.

Question 5: That we would know His love as irrisistable.

Question 6: Many possible answers, but grasping God's love and goodness, as Ruth saw in Naomi, is principal.

Question 7: Some applicable verses for the 4 pledges:

Pledge 1: II Corinthians 5:17; Ephesians 4:24; Matthew 19:27

Pledge 2: Philippians 3:13-14; Matthew 8:20

Pledge 3: Ephesians 2:13-16; Luke 14:25-33

Pledge 4: Luke 9:62; I John 3:16

## LESSON 3
NAOMI'S FACE

Question 1: Much like the prodigal son, she is loved and was missed.

Question 2: Naomi, like she says, is bitter and also sad. Significance? The truth of leaving behind Bethlehem (God) and going to Moab (the world) was not so great.

Question 3: She was received with love, acceptance and listening ears. Just what she needed.

HONESTY

Question 1: How can God help and change our circumstances if we are not honest? Naomi couldn't say, "God is good" at the moment because she didn't yet know God as good to her.

Question 2: Our relationship with Christ is to be real. Some do not understand God's compassionate heart and that He is near the broken hearted. They need to realize God cares and desires we cry out to Him.
Question 3: Discuss why you chose your answer. The Truth? God has just brought Naomi home to bless her!

ITS BARLEY HARVEST TIME
Jeremiah 25:4-11 explains why God sends His people into captivity.
Question 1: God always has a heart to bless those coming to Him.
Question 2: Sometimes, we have the wrong impression of God, that He is harsh and can't forgive us. But this is not true.
Question 3: No answer is incorrect.
Question 4: Time to share blessings from God you weren't expecting. Example: My husband is my barley field. I didn't know what a true man of God he was at first. I thought he was a field with not much barley. It took some work and God humbling me for my eyes to be opened to the beauty of him and what he is in God. I am thankful for him very much. He is my barley field!

CLOSING
Question 1: The Jews despised the Moabites and it was even Jewish law that they could not marry one. However, though Ruth was a new convert, the people didn't know this yet.

**LESSON 4**
For this lesson, it would be good to understand how the barley harvest process works and its eight stages:
1. The men cut the barley.
2. The women bind the barley into sheaves.
3. Gleaning (collecting) is done on what is left behind.
4. The sheaves are transported to the threshing floor.
5. Threshing the barley: loosening the grain from the straw, usually by being treaded upon by cattle or by use of a toothed threshing sledge.
6. Winnowing the barley: tossing the grain into the air. The wind blows away the chaff and straw.

7. The grain is sifted to remove any residual.
8. The grain is bagged for storage or transportation.

Various analogies of the eight stages of harvest and the Christian's walk:
1. God will sometimes empty us.
2. He will get us where he wants us when he wants.
3. We should let nothing be lost or wasted – the gospel is for all people.
4. Trials come our way to shake us up and move us about and make us Christ-like.
5. Trials are meant to improve our character.
6. Refining is a process making us more Christ-like.
7. More refining fine tunes us – again – to be like Christ.
8. Now we can be a blessing.

The Law of Gleaning:
Farmers were not to harvest the corners of their fields but leave grain for the poor to collect. (Lev. 19:9; Lev. 23:22). The farmer who does this, the Lord promises to bless. (Dt. 24:19). Ruth was willing to take advantage of this law, but she was also aware that not all the farmers followed the law, or followed it but not in a right spirit.

BOAZ
Question 1: Boaz is Elimilech's relative (in a position to bless) and is very wealthy.
Question 2: Jesus, our brother, is rich and willing to give up everything for us; Jesus, on the cross, has made us rich and blesses us; In Christ we are given a great inheritance.

DIRECTED FOOTSTEPS
Question 1: No wrong answers
Question 2: She hoped to find favor rather than trouble. She was aware of the dangers as a gleaner.
Question 3: The needy and those in hard times. We should never forget them.
Question 4: Open for sharing.

## A GOOD RECOMMENDATION
<u>Question 1:</u> There will be many answers to this question. One might be that he walks the talk.
<u>Question 2:</u> She is connected to Naomi. She asked permission to glean. She is a hard worker. Boaz wants to know her character.
<u>Question 3:</u> Ways God favors us: unexpected blessings, answered prayers, open doors, provision, etc.

## HIS WORDS
<u>Question 1:</u> $2^{nd}$ application: He guides our paths. $3^{rd}$ application: He gives living water to those who thirst for Him.
<u>Question 2:</u> We seed refuge in God; we love His name; we are His child; we listen, watch and wait for God.

## REASON FOR GOD'S GRACE
<u>Question 1:</u> Because of Ruth's sacrifice and loyalty to Naomi. Also, she left mother and father and she came to a foreign land.
<u>Question 2:</u> (Psalm 5) when we depend on Him and love Him. (John 1) Nothing more than being His child causes Him to favor us. (Proverbs 8) When we listen, obey and focus on Him.

More about favor:
<u>Genesis 4:4</u> Abel was favored because he honored God.
<u>Exodus 33:12-16</u> Favor to Moses was God's granted presence. "If you are pleased with me," he says, "teach me your ways that I may know you and continue to find favor with you."
<u>Esther 7:3</u> Favor with the king meant life, not death. Meant one was allowed to come into his presence when they so desired.
<u>Luke 1:30</u> Mary was highly favored. Thus she was chosen by God.
<u>Psalm 90:17</u> Favor is when the beauty of the Lord is on you and your labors are blessed.
<u>Proverbs 8:35</u> Life and his presence is favor.
<u>Proverbs 18:22</u> Favor is being blessed with a good spouse.

## A BLESSING PRAYER
<u>Question 3:</u> We must allow it and we must run to Him.

## LESSON 5

A kinsman-redeemer is responsible for protecting the interests of a needy member of the extended family by -

1.  Providing an heir for a dead brother (Dt. 25:5-10).
2.  Redeeming land that a poor relative will have to sell outside the family (Lev. 25:25-28).
3.  Redeeming a relative that had been sold to slavery (Lev. 25:47-49).
4.  Avenge the killing of a relative.

Rahab: Boaz's mother was Rahab, a prostitute from Jericho. Read about her in Joshua 2, Joshua 6:20-25, Matthew 1:5, James 2:5 and Hebrews 11:31. She was applauded for her great faith. Having Rahab for his mother, Boaz, was open to a gentile believer such as Ruth.

Question 2: Boaz accepted Ruth, his workers will too because he invited her to eat with them. Small talk happens around a meal; we get comfortable with one another.

Question 3: Possibly – she is one of us, or – please, extend her grace.

Question 4: Possibly because He is abundant in all giving and grace. Many answers possible for this question.

Question 5:– He wishes to bless her. He is expressing favor and also reward for her treatment of Naomi.

Question 6: Boaz is an example of the love and character of Christ - mighty in pedigree, mighty in power, has total authority and is rich in grace.

WORKING TOGETHER

Question 1: Boaz is requesting different and better treatment of Ruth than they would give another. She is to be given respect and honor.

Question 2: Ruth is being blessed though she did not plant the crops. She is being blessed because God loves her. All God's children are to rejoice together and bask in God's love, together.

ABUNDANCE AND SHARING

Question 1: He is going to bless her and is blessing her.

## LESSON 6

Bride and Bridegroom reference in the scriptures:

As a bridegroom rejoices over his bride, so will your God rejoice over you. (Isaiah 62:5b)

The friend (John the Baptist) who attends the bridegroom (Jesus) waits and listens for him and is full of joy when he hears the bridegroom's voice. (John 3:29)

## A PLAN

Question 2: Maybe Naomi knew that Boaz had fallen in love with Ruth. On an additional note, Jesus, our redeemer, was not obligated to go to the Cross for us. He had free will. The Father was confident Jesus would be our redeemer because He knew love would win out.

## PREPARATION

Question 1: To wash, anoint herself and dress in her best. To present herself holy for him. Applying this to ourselves: our sins are washed away, we are anointed with the Holy Spirit, we will wear robes of white, made white by the blood of the Lamb.

Question 2: Titus 3:5: We are not clean because of our own righteousness but by His mercy, He washes us clean. Ephesians 5:26: We are washed by Christ who makes us holy.

Question 3: An aroma of obedience (to Naomi), love and loyalty, submission, etc.

Question 4: The righteous acts of God's holy people

Question 5: Ruth – to go to the threshing floor that night, in faith. Rahab – she hid Israel's spies.

Question 6: Ruth was a Moabite (non-Jew) but cleansed (converted) for a noble purpose. Rahab was a prostitute and non-Jew, also cleansed for a noble purpose. The lineage of Christ the Messiah comes through Rahab and Ruth.

## APPROPRIATING GOD'S WORD

What is appropriation? If you are a Christian you have appropriated; you have appropriated salvation through Jesus Christ, personally, for yourself. Salvation is offered to all, but it is only realized when we appropriate it, personally. We also appropriate things like physical healing, deliverance, gifts of the Spirit, etc. To appropriate is to receive it for yourself, personally.

Question 1: We are to ask Christ into our hearts. He wants us to want Him. We are to appropriate salvation – Ruth is appropriating the kinsmen-redeemer law.

Question 2: Humilty maybe. Our acknowledging we need Him.

Question 3: Talk about the heart of Boaz and Christ, that they would selflessly be a redeemer. Love drives us to sacrifice for someone. The law does not.

Question 4: Grace is unearned favor. Grace is a gift, given freely. Grace reflects the love of the giver of the grace.

Question 5: To submit to Christ is to take on His name, acknowledge He is our help and our salvation. Christ protects us (from the evil one and the lawy) by making us His, taking us under His wings.

DEEPER

Question 1: Christ fulfills the law; He will stand behind all His promises to us.

Question 2: Mt. 6:33 – The promise is God will take care of our basic needs. The condition is that we seek Him and His righteousness first – He is our first priority. Isaiah 43:1-2 – The promise is God will supernaturally get us through hard things. The condition is to not fear but to trust Him. James 4:8 – The promise is God will come near to us and the condition is that we draw near to Him, approach Him. Romans 8:28 – the promise is that God will bring good out of all things for us. The condition is that we are His (we love Him).

CLOSING

Question 1: Servant: Christ came to serve but we also serve Him. The same as with Boaz and Ruth. Friend: We can call Jesus, the son of God, our friend. He calls us His friend. He not only loves us, He likes us. Wife/Husband: The Bride-Bridegroom relationship is an intimate one. Involves a deeper commitment.

**LESSON 7**

BOAZ'S RESPONSE

Question 1: Ruth: Noble, not self-consumed, a bit nervous. Boaz: He (v. 14) cares about Ruth's reputation. He is gentle. (v. 11). He has integrity (v 12). He goes beyond his obligation. (v. 15).

Question 2: Possibly, Ruth looked fearful. Or he could be saying, have faith.

Question 3: It means there will be no punishment to her for this act of faith. God is good and He will prove it. Ruth's new God is not a punishing God.

THE TEST

Question 1: Doubts might be riddling Ruth. Fear tormenting her. Or she may have been at peace. How would we be, though?

Question 2: Boaz might have been relieved there was someone else and shown his relief, caring only about himself and his money.

Question 3: Boaz is a man of God and will *submit* to the laws of God. Because of that, he has faith in God for Ruth, that all will turn out good for her and himself.

Question 4: The other redeemer does not have his own heart invested with Ruth. He is calculating and practical, no emotion except for his own welfare.

Question 5: This is only speculation on our part.

Question 7: Boaz's faith is strong enough that he himself can sleep even when things are uncertain. His words to Ruth could be: God will show Himself full of love and grace toward you, Ruth. Hope in God more than me.

ENCOURAGEMENT

Question 1: Boaz is concerned for Ruth's reputation and wishes it to remain pure.

Question 3: It means we will not be disappointed in God. Ever. We are to trust this fact, that He is for us and not against us. We must trust His love is good.

Question 4: Boaz, giving her the barley, was a seal of his good intent, his word, and his faith in God. The Holy Spirit, God's seal on us, reminds us we are His and will always be His. We need not worry for

99

God is close and within. The parrallel: Both promise their love and care for eternity.

NAOMI'S WISDOM

Question 1: Naomi, like Boaz, has faith. She is telling Ruth to have faith and do not worry, but see what God will do.

**LESSON 8**

Scripture preparation

Matthew 5:17. Boaz will in a way, abolish the law, (other kinsmen-redeemer) by stepping in.

Romans 7:4. Ruth's fruit is the eventual birth of the Messiah in her family tree; our gift of grace fulfilling the law.

Romans 8:3. The other kinsmen-redeemer was powerless to help Ruth because he was not willing to sacrifice

Romans 13:8 Love fulfills the law.

II Corinthians 5:14-15 Love is the motivator.

Galatians 3:25. Ruth is set free from the other kinsmen-redeemer.

The city gate: A city gate served as an administrative and judicial center where legal matters were discussed and prosecuted. Witnesses were readily available as we see in the book of Ruth. We could compare this to our town hall.

Redemption: Throughout the Old Testament we find the theme of redemption. First born sons, first born animals and land are redeemed. The purpose of redemption is that something is returned to its original state. In Ruth, the land is to be redeemed and accounted as belonging to her deceased husband's family. The purpose is to keep the name of the deceased alive in Israel by seeing it remains in the historical records. To be taken from the book is to have your name blotted out. So our names are written in the Book of Life, never to be blotted out, because Christ redeemed us. Redemption leads to *eternal* life. We become joint heirs of the kingdom of God with Christ by redemption.

## MEETING WITH THE UNNAMED RELATIVE

Question 1: This law takes care of the destitute, however it ignores love. Or does it, since it is not obligation?

Question 2: It reflects his respect and love for Ruth and that she would be worried until this was settled. It reflects the integrity of Boaz.

Question 3: The purpose of the law is to lead us to Christ. The unnamed relative leads Boaz to Ruth and Ruth to Boaz for they had to pass through him first.

## DIPLOMACY

Question 1: The goal of being diplomatic is to come to a peaceful resolution without a fight or discord arising. In the end, everyone is happy.

Question 2: Tact and diplomatic skills are sensitive to the other person's opinions and feelings. It is not presuring or rushing someone to make a decision. Boaz is making sure the relative considers one step at a time, that a rash decision would not be made.

## THE SMALL PRINT

Question 1: He will have to marry a Moabite and his estate will go to her first husband's family.

Question 3 and 4: The purpose of the unnamed relative is to open a door for Boaz. So, the law leads us to Christ. Also, the purpose of the relative, and the law, is to reveal the immense love of Boaz has for Ruth. He is willing to sacrifice while the other relative would not. The message to us is God's great love for us, no matter the cost.

## THE LAW VS CHRIST

Question 2: All have sinned and fall short of fulfilling the law. Heaven is impossible without a redeemer. Christ is that redeemer for us. Without Him, we are doomed and have not hope. Because Christ loves me, He redeems me.

## THE CONTRACT IS SEALED

Question 1: To strive to be perfect work for acceptance. The law is burdensome and hard.

Question 2: _Christ gave up his life for us. The Cross expresses His full commitment and love for us.

Question 3: alive with Christ; forgave my sins; the law that would convict me; nailed; disarmed; triumphed.

Question 4: We no longer need to fear condemnation and death.

Question 5: Ruth no longer need fear destitution and uncertaintity of her future. She no longer needs to fear being entangled with the other relative – representing the law.

## LESSON 9
### PUBLIC PROCLAMATION

Question 1: He proclaims he has redeemed Naomi and all her property and that he has acquired Ruth, the Moabite. He makes this a public proclamation so it can not be disputed. The Cross was a very public proclamation as well.

Question 2: The result is that the family name of Elimilech is preservded in the records of his family. This will affect all the descendents of Elimilech. But we will also see, it will affect all of Israel.

Question 3: Their name is blotted out of the records. They are forgotten.

Question 4: See Dt. 7:9 God keeps his covenant of love to a thousand generations of those who love him. Our responsibility? To love the Lord and pass on his blessing to our descendants.

### THE BOOK OF LIFE

This is the roster of believers....the names of the elect. It is a book we want our name in! To NOT be in this book is to be one who will not be saved. In Israel, ownership of the land by families was of utmost importance, putting your name in their book. And it was important to keep the family name going through land ownership being passed down to the children. For a family to lose their land and not have it redeemed, was a horrible thing; the family name would disappear from the records forever. We are a kind of land - God's. He redeems us and keeps puts our name in His Book of Life. It is there forever for He will never lose us, never die!

Question 1: We inherit eternal life with God.
Question 2: Psalm 111: His covenant with us is forever; Psalm 37: God's hand is holding us up that we will not fall though we may stumble
Question 3: Because this nation of Jews are family. Tightly knit.
Question 5: God will not lose us but He keeps us. If we truly love Him, know Him, we are assured. Do you know Him?

## BLESSINGS
## THE FIRST BLESSING
Question 1: The blessing is that Ruth would be like Rachel and Leah, who built up the family of Israel. Rachel and Leah were the two wives of Jacob (Jacob later named Israel) from whom the 12 tribes (12 sons) of Israel came. (12 sons came from Rachael, Leah and their two handmaidens.)
Question 2: Possibly, they think long term, of the generations to come, and the survival of a their nation. And they are a people always looking for their Messiah.
Question 3: Knowing Christ and seeing our family come to faith as well.

## THE SECOND BLESSING
Question 1: May you have standing in Ephrathah and be famous in Bethlehem. Ephrathah is the area around Bethlehem.
Question 2: Yes. Boaz is the great grandfather of David. The Messiah, a descendent of Boaz and Ruth. Boaz is always mentioned in the lineage of Jesus Christ.
Question 3: To be of good standing is that we stand forgiven before God. We are His child and related to the Christ.

## THE THIRD BLESSING
Question 1: May your family be like that of Perez, whom Tamar bore to Judah.

Perez led his tribe to prominence among the 11 other tribes. Through Perez the tribe of Judah gained good standing in Israel. Perez is an ancestor of Boaz.

Question 2: They are thinking of the whole nation of Israel.

Tamar initiated redemption as Ruth initiated redemption. She was the wife, first of Er, the eldest son of Judah, then of Onan his brother (after Er died.) Both sons left her without an heir. Their father, Judah, promised her that when his other son, Shelah, grew up, he would fill the kinsman-redeemer position. However, Judah did not stand by his word. Tamar, in disguise, prostituted herself with Judah, became pregnant and bore twins, Perez and Zarah.

Question 3: We are given rest from working for salvation. God assures we will not be destroyed or taken by the enemy.

Other nations wanted to make Israel extinct. Peace in Israel has always been, and still is, a longing.

Peace and rest in the land: Look at Israel's past and present – all the battles are about land. Joshua was told to go and take the land. If you've fought for something, shed blood for something, you won't easily give it up.

Jesus fought for us in that he bled, suffered and died. Through the finished work of the cross he redeemed us - purchased us back. So, why would he easily give us up to the enemy?

APPLICATION
Question 1: security and peace in the relationship might be one answer.
Question 2: Typically, we don't think outside our immediate family.

BEYOND SELF
Question 1: Naomi. The Nation Israel. The whole world.

Question 3: They thought of themselves as a whole more than individuals. They were connected having one God. God's enemy's were theirs.

## LESSON 10
FRUITFULNESS IN MARRIAGE
Question 1: Ruth had been barren but God enabled her to conceive with Boaz. For the redemption to be complete, Ruth needed to have a son. God saw that that happened.
Question 2: God chooses us and appoints us to bear fruit.
Question 3: Fruit is good for us and the different varieties delight our taste buds.
Question 4: That we produce fruit is for the health of the body of Christ as well.

FRUITFULNESS BEYOND RUTH AND BOAZ
Question 1: They are thanking God for the birth of Obed.
Question 2: Their respect of us might be increased. They might expect to know more of the famous person through us. They would have questions for us.
Question 3: We should pray our children know Christ.
Question 4: Naomi now has hope for her future. Life is now good for her. She will be cared for the rest of her life.
Question 5: To be restored is to now be strong, firm and steady.
Question 6: Joy. Soul.
Question 7: Love is always God's motivation.
Question 8: Christ carries us, helps us. His Word also helps and sustains us.

FRUITFULNESS FOR ALL
Question 1: Based on Ruth's love for Naomi and her sacrificial way of loving throughout the story, we can probably assume Ruth is happy with all this.
Question 2: Again, it is community and love for all.

Question 3: It is an honor to be a servant of God, but they may be thinking of some amazing servants in the past: Perez, Moses, Abraham.

TWO FAMILY TREES
Question 1: Redemption; Boaz and Ruth.
Question 2: Joseph; Mary. God. Jesus was born in order to redeem us.

APPLICATION
Question 1: The common good implies they are not to be kept selfishly but exercised for others. It is not about us.
Question 2: In the church.
Question 3: We ask for the gifts and do so because we want to bless others with them.
Question 4: We can encourage others to use their gifts too. We can give them opportunity for it.

# OTHER BOOKS YOU MIGHT ENJOY
## BY PATSY SCOTT

BETWEEN PORCH AND ALTAR: Intercessory Prayers and Teaching for the Prayer Closet.

QUESTIONS JESUS ASKED: A 25-day devotional to stir your spirit and fine-tune your spiritual ears.

A HOUSE OF PRAYER: Powering up –Sweeping out – Surrendering: 21 days of Meditation and Prayer.

LIVING IN END TIMES: Preparation for the Day of the Lord.

THE POWER OF LOVE: 8 Bible-Based Lessons for Individual or Group Study. (Based on Part I of *Living in End Times*.)

THE POWER TO STAND FIRM: 8 Bible-Based Lessons for Individual or Group Study. (Based on Part II of *Living in End Times*.)

THE POWER OF CONSECRATION: 7 Bible-Based Lessons for Individual or Group Study. (Based on Part III of *Living in End Times*.)

THE POWER OF KNOWING: 8 Bible-Based Lessons for Individual or Group Study. (Based on Part IV of *Living in End Times*.)

JAMES: Living a Blessed Life. A Bible Study on the Book of James.

JUDGE NOT: The Sin and Repercussions of Judging.